THE SECRET OF UNITED PRAYER

THE SECRET OF
UNITED PRAYER

Andrew Murray

CLC PUBLICATIONS
Fort Washington, PA 19034

The Secret of United Prayer
Published by CLC Publications

USA: P.O. Box 1449, Fort Washington, PA 19034
www.clcpublications.com

UK: Kingsway CLC Trust
Unit 5, Glendale Avenue, Sandycroft, Flintshire, CH5 2QP
www.equippingthechurch.com

This printing 2025

Printed in the United States of America

ISBN (trade paper): 978-1-61958-272-9
ISBN (e-book): 978-1-61958-273-6

Italics in Scripture quotations are the emphasis of the author.

Cover design by Mitch Bolton.

FOREWORD

DURING the last years of my father's life he thought much on the subject of united prayer and about a Prayer Union for all saints. Some few years ago he began such a Prayer Union in Dutch, which since his homegoing in 1917 has been called the "Andrew Murray Prayer Union." The only condition of membership was that anyone desirous of joining should write, sending in his name as a sign of a real desire for prayer in unison with others. The thoughts embodied in this booklet are some to which my father gave prominence and which occupied his mind up to the very end. May God graciously grant his desire and ours that many will join the ranks of intercessors—those who pray continually for the church of Christ and His kingdom on earth.

ANDREW MURRAY

Day 1

The Lost Secret

Wait for the Promise of the Father. . . . You shall be baptized with the Holy Spirit not many days from now.

Acts 1:4–5

AFTER our Lord had given the Great Commission, "Go into all the world and preach the gospel to every creature" (Mark 16:15), He again added another, His very last command: "Tarry . . . until you are endued with power from on high" (Luke 24:49). And He elaborated: "You shall be baptized with the Holy Spirit not many days from now."

All Christians agree that the great command to preach the gospel to every creature was not only for the disciples but is binding on us too. But many do not appear to consider that the very last command—*not* to preach until they had received the power from on high—is also as binding on us as it was on the disciples. The church appears to have lost possession of that which ought to be to her a secret of secrets—the abiding consciousness, day by day, that it is only as she lives in the power of the Holy Spirit that she can preach the gospel in demonstration of the Spirit and of power. It is owing to this lack that there is so much preaching and working with so little spiritual result. Along with this is the widespread fact that there is so little consistent prayer—and especially that there is so little of that much-availing prayer which brings down the power from on high upon her ministrations.

In this little book we desire to study the secret of Pentecost as it is to be found in the words and the deeds of our blessed Master, and in the words and the deeds of His disciples as they took Him at His word and continued with one accord in prayer and supplication until the promise was fulfilled and they became full of the Holy Spirit and proved what the mighty power of their God could do through them.

Let us seek earnestly the grace of the Holy Spirit, who alone can reveal to us what eye has not seen, nor ear heard, nor has entered into the heart of man to conceive (see 1 Cor. 2:9)—the things which God has done and loves to do for those who wait upon Him. Let us pray that the lost secret may be found—the sure promise that in answer to fervent prayer the power of the Holy Spirit will indeed be given.

Day 2

The Kingdom of God

[Jesus] also presented Himself alive [to His apostles] . . . being seen by them during forty days and speaking of the things pertaining to the kingdom of God.

Acts 1:3

WHEN Christ began to preach He took up the message of John: "The kingdom of heaven is at hand" (Matt. 3:2). Later on He declared: "There are some standing here who will not taste death till they see the kingdom of God present with power" (Mark 9:1). That could not be until the King had ascended His throne. Only then were He and His disciples ready to receive from the Father the great gift of the Holy Spirit, bringing down the kingdom of God in its heavenly power into their hearts.

Our text tells us that all the teaching of Jesus during the forty days after the resurrection dealt with the kingdom of God, and it is remarkable how Luke, in the last verses of Acts, sums up all the teaching of Paul at Rome: he testified to the kingdom of God; he preached the kingdom of God (see Acts 28:23, 31).

Christ seated upon the throne of God was now King and Lord of all. To His disciples He had entrusted the announcement of the kingdom which is righteousness and peace and joy in the Holy Spirit. The prayer He had taught them, "Our Father in heaven . . . Your kingdom come" (Matt. 6:9–10), had now for them a new meaning. The rule of God as seen in heaven came down in the power of the Spirit, and the disciples were full of one thought: to preach concerning the coming of the Spirit into the hearts of men. There was now on earth good tidings of the kingdom of God, a kingdom of God ruling and dwelling with men, even as in heaven.

In the last command our Lord gave to His disciples (see Acts 1:4, 8) we shall find the essential characteristics of the kingdom clearly set forth.

1. The King—the crucified Christ. 2. The disciples—His faithful followers. 3. The power for their service—the Holy Spirit. 4. Their work—testifying for Christ as His witnesses. 5. Their aim—the ends of the earth. 6. Their first duty—waiting on God in united, unceasing prayer.

If we are to take up and continue the prayer of the disciples, it is essential to have a clear and full impression of all that Christ said to them in that last moment, and what it meant for their inner life and all their service.

Day 3

Christ is King

And He said to them, "Assuredly, I say to you that there are some standing here who will not taste death till they see the kingdom of God present with power."

Mark 9:1

THE first mark of the church: Christ is King. Christ and John had both preached that the kingdom of God was at hand. In our text, Christ said that it would be in the lifetime of some who heard Him that the kingdom would come in power. That could mean nothing else but that when He, as King, had ascended to the throne of the Father, the kingdom would be revealed in the hearts of His disciples by the power of the Holy Spirit. In the kingdom in *heaven*, God's will was always being done; in the power of the Holy Spirit, Christ's disciples would do His will even as it was done in heaven.

The mark of what a kingdom is, is to be seen in its *King*. Christ now reigns as God and man on the throne of the Father. On earth there is no embodiment or external manifestation of the kingdom; its power is seen in the lives of those in whom it rules. It is only in the church, the members of Christ, that the united body can be seen and known. Christ lives and dwells and rules in their hearts. Our Lord Himself taught how close the relationship would be. "At that day you will know that I am in My Father, and you in Me, and I in you" (John14:20).

Next to their faith about His oneness with God and their trust in His omnipotent power would be the knowledge that *they lived in Him and He in them.*

Here is our first lesson if we are to follow in the steps of the disciples and to share their blessing: we must know that Christ *as King* actually dwells and rules in our hearts. We must know that we live in Him and that in His power we are able to accomplish all He would have us do. Our whole life is to be devoted to our King and the service of His kingdom.

This blessed relationship to Christ will mean, above all, a daily fellowship with Him in prayer. The prayer life is to be a continuous and unbroken exercise. It is thus that His people can rejoice in their King and in Him can be more than conquerors.

Day 4

Jesus the Crucified

God has made this Jesus, whom you crucified, both Lord and Christ.

Acts 2:36

WE have spoken of Christ as King in more than one respect. But there is one fact more that must not be overlooked. This King is none other than the crucified Jesus. All that we have to say about Him—His divine power, His abiding presence, His wonderful love—does not teach us to know Him aright unless we maintain the deep consciousness: This our King is the *crucified Jesus*. God has placed Him in the midst of His throne as a Lamb, looking as if it had been slain, and it is thus that the hosts of heaven adore Him. It is thus that we worship Him as a King.

Christ's cross is His highest glory. It is through this that He has conquered every enemy and gained His place on the throne of God. And it is this condition of death that He will impart to us too, if we are to know fully what the victory over sin is to mean. When Paul wrote: "I have been crucified with Christ . . . Christ lives in me" (Gal. 2:20), he taught us that it was as the *crucified* One that Christ ruled on the throne of his heart, and that the spirit of the cross should triumph over us as it did in him.

This was true of the disciples. This was their deepest preparation for receiving the Holy Spirit; they had, with their Lord, been crucified to the world. The old man had been crucified: in Him they were dead to sin and their life was hid with Christ in God (see Col. 3:3). Each one of us needs to experience this fellowship with Christ *in His cross* if the Spirit of Pentecost is really to take possession of us. It was through the eternal Spirit that Christ gave Himself as a sacrifice and became the King on the throne of God. It is as we become "conformed to His death" (Phil. 3:10)—in the entire surrender of our will, in the entire self-denial of our old nature, in the entire separation from the spirit of this world—that we can become the worthy servants of a crucified King and our hearts the worthy temples of His glory.

Day 5

The Apostles

Being assembled together with them, He commanded them not to depart from Jerusalem, but to wait for the Promise of the Father.

Acts 1:4

THE second mark of the church is to be found in *the disciples* whom the Lord had prepared to receive His Spirit and to be His witnesses.

If we would understand aright the outpouring of the Spirit in answer to the prayer of the disciples, we must above all ask: What was there in these men that fitted them for such powerful, effective prayer and the wonderful fulfillment of the promise that came to them? They were simple, unlearned men with many faults, whom the Lord had called to forsake all and follow Him. They had done this, as far as they could; they followed Him in the life He led and the work He did. Though there was much sin in them, and they had as yet no power fully to deny themselves, their hearts clung to Him in deep sincerity. In the midst of much stumbling they yet followed Him to the cross. They shared with Him His death; unconsciously, but most really, they *died with Him* to sin and were *raised with Him* in the power of a new life. It was *this* that fitted them for that power in prayer and for their being clothed with the power from on high.

Let this be the test by which we try ourselves: whether *we* have indeed surrendered to the fellowship of Christ's sufferings and death, and whether *we* have hated our own life and crucified it and have received the power of Christ's life in us. It is *this* that will give us liberty to believe that God will hear our prayer too, and give us His Holy Spirit to work in us what we and He desire—if we are indeed with one accord to take up the disciples' prayer and to share in the answer. We must, like them, be willing learners in the school of Jesus and seek above everything that intimate fellowship with Him which will fit us for praying the prayer of Pentecost and receiving its answer.

Day 6

Not of This World

They are not of the world, just as I am not of the world.
John 17:14, 16

ON that last night our Lord took pains to make clear to His disciples the impassable gulf between Him and the world, and between them and the world too (see John 17:6–21). He had said of the Spirit: "The world cannot receive [Him], because it neither sees Him nor knows Him" (John 14:17). And of them: "You are not of the world . . . therefore the world hates you" (John 15:19).

One great mark of the disciples was thus to be that as little as Christ was of the world, so little were *they* to be of the world. Christ and they had become united in the cross and the resurrection; they both belonged to another world, the kingdom of heaven. This separation from the world is to be the mark of all disciples who long to be filled with the Spirit.

How is it that faith in the Holy Spirit is so little preached and practiced in Christendom? The world rules too much in the life of Christians. Christians live too little the heavenly life to which they are called in Christ Jesus. The "love of the world" (see 1 John 2:15–16); "the lust of the flesh," pleasure in eating and drinking, in ease and comfort; "the lust of the eyes," delight in all that the world offers of beauty and possession "the pride of life," self-exaltation in what the wisdom and power of man has accomplished—all this robs the heart of its susceptibility and desire for that true self-denial that fits a person for receiving the Holy Spirit.

Let each one who would take up the Pentecostal prayer for the power of the Holy Spirit examine himself as to whether the spirit of the world is not the reason for that lack of love of prayer which is absolutely necessary in all who would plead the promise of the Father. May the Lord write this deep in every heart: *The world cannot receive the Holy Spirit!* "[You] are not of the world, just as I am not of the world" (John 17:16).

Day 7

Obedience

If you love Me, keep My commandments. And I will pray the Father, and He will give you another Helper.

John 14:15–16

WE have come to know the disciples in their training for the baptism of the Spirit and have seen what was needed for their continuing "with one accord" in the prayer for the power of the Spirit. Christ was everything to them. Even before the cross, but much more after it and the resurrection, He was literally their life, their one thought, their only desire.

Such a devotion to Christ—was this something special and not to be expected of all? Or is it indeed something that the Lord asks from all who desire to be filled with the Spirit? God expects it of *all* His children. The Lord has need of such now, as much as then, to receive His Spirit and His power, to minister His grace on earth, and, as intercessors, to link the world to the throne of God.

Is Christ something or nothing or everything to us? For the unconverted, Christ is nothing; for the half-converted, the average Christian—Christ is something; for the true Christian, Christ is *all*. Each one who prays for the power of the Spirit must be ready to say: "I yield myself with my whole heart this day to the leading of the Spirit." A full surrender becomes a question of life or death, an absolute necessity.

My dear brother, my dear sister, you have heard the word of our text: "If you love Me, *keep My commandments.*" The surrender to live every day, all the day, abiding in Christ and keeping His commandments, is to be the one mark of your discipleship. It is then the child of God learns that it is only as the heart longs in everything to do God's will that the Father's love and Spirit can rest upon it. This was the disposition in which the disciples continued with one accord in prayer. This will be the secret of power in our intercession as we plead for the church and the world.

Day 8

The Holy Spirit

You shall be baptized with the Holy Spirit. . . . You shall receive power when the Holy Spirit has come upon you.

Acts 1:5, 8

THE third mark of the church: *the power for service through the Holy Spirit.* Since the time of Adam's fall—when he lost the spirit God had breathed into him—God's Spirit had striven with men and worked in some with power, but He had never been able to find His permanent home in them.

It was only when Christ had come, and by His death had broken the power of sin and in the resurrection had won a new life for men to live in Himself, that the Spirit of God could come and take possession of the whole heart and make it a dwelling for Christ and for God.

Nothing less than this could be the power in the disciples and in us by which sin could be overcome and the prisoners set free. This Spirit is the *Holy Spirit.* In the Old Testament He was called the Spirit of God. But now that in the cross of Christ the *holiness* of God had been magnified and Christ had through the cross sanctified them and us that we might be set apart like Him; now on the day of Pentecost the Spirit of God's *holiness* descends to dwell in men and take possession of them as God's holy temple.

He is also the Spirit *of the Son.* On earth He led the Son first into the desert to be tempted by Satan, then to the synagogue in Nazareth to proclaim Himself as the fulfillment of what the prophets had spoken (see Isa. 61:1; Luke 4:18). And so daily, on to the cross, Christ yielded Himself implicitly to the leading of the Spirit.

The Spirit now reveals Christ in us as first of all our life, and then our strength, for a perfect obedience and the preaching of the Word in the power of God.

Amazing mystery! The Spirit of God, our life; the Spirit of Christ, our light and strength. It is as men and women led by this Spirit who guided the first disciples that we shall have the power to pray the effective prayer of the righteous man that avails much (see James 5:16).

Day 9

The Power from on High

Tarry . . . until you are endued with power from on high.
Luke 24:49

THE Lord had said to the disciples: "Without Me you can do nothing" (John 15:5). Why then is it that He has chosen these impotent, helpless men and sent them out to conquer the world for Him? It was that in their *feebleness* they might yield themselves and give Him, as Lord, the opportunity on His throne to show His power working through them. As the Father had done all the work in Christ when He was upon earth, so Christ in heaven would now be the Great Worker, proving in them that all power had been given to Him in heaven and on earth. Their place would be to pray, to believe, and to yield themselves to the mighty power of Christ.

The Holy Spirit would not be in them as a power of which *they* could have possession. But He would possess *them*, and their work would be in very deed the work of the almighty Christ. Their whole posture each day would be that of unceasing dependence and prayer, and of confident expectation.

The apostles had indeed learned to know Christ intimately. They had seen all His mighty works; they had received His teaching; they had gone with Him through all His sufferings, even to His death on the cross. They had not only seen Him but known Him in the power of

His resurrection and the experience of that resurrection life in their own hearts. Yet they were not capable of making Him known aright until He Himself, from the throne of heaven, had taken possession of them by His Spirit dwelling in them.

Everything calls the gospel minister to rest content with nothing less than the indwelling life and power of the Holy Spirit revealing *Jesus* in the heart as the only fitness for preaching the gospel in power. Nothing less than having Christ speaking through us in the power of His omnipotence will make us able ministers of the New Testament, bringing salvation to those who hear us.

Day 10

My Witnesses

You shall be witnesses to Me.

Acts 1:8

THE fourth mark of Christ's church: His servants are to be witnesses to Him, ever testifying of His wonderful love, of His power to redeem, of His continual abiding presence, and of His wonderful power to work in them.

This is the only weapon that the King allows His redeemed ones to use. Without claiming authority or power, without wisdom or eloquence, without influence or position, each one is called, not only by his words but by his life and action, to be *a living witness to and proof of what Jesus can do.*

This is to be the only weapon they are to use in conquering men and bringing them to the feet of Christ. This is what the first disciples did. When they were filled with the Spirit they began to speak of the mighty things that *Christ* had done.

It was in this power that those who were scattered abroad by persecution went forth, even as far as Antioch, preaching in the name of Jesus—so that a multitude of the heathen believed. They had no commission from the apostles; they had no special gifts or training—but out of the fullness of the heart they spoke of Jesus Christ! They could not be silent; they were filled with the life and the love of Christ and could not but witness to Him.

It was this that gave the gospel its power of increase: every new convert became a *witness* for Christ.

A heathen writer tells later, in regard to the persecutions, that if the Christians had been content to keep the worship of Jesus to themselves they would not have had to suffer. But in their zeal they wanted Christ to rule over all.

Here we have the secret of a flourishing church: *every believer a witness for Jesus*. Here we have the cause of the weakness of the church: so few who are willing in daily life to testify that Jesus is Lord.

What a call to prayer! Lord, teach Your disciples the blessedness of knowing Jesus and the power of His love, that they may find their highest joy in witnessing to what He is and has done for them.

The Gospel Ministry

The Spirit of truth . . . He will testify of Me. And you also will bear witness, because you have been with Me from the beginning.

John 15:26–27

"MY witnesses"—that not only refers to all believers but very specially to all ministers of the gospel. This is the high calling and also the only power of the preacher of the gospel—*in everything to be a witness for Jesus.*

This gives us two great truths. The first, that whatever the preacher teaches from the Word of God, and whatever may be the need of his congregation, he must put first of all the preaching about Christ Himself. This is what the first disciples did. "In every house, they did not cease teaching and preaching Jesus as the Christ" (Acts 5:42). This was what Philip did at Samaria. "[He] preached Christ to them" (8:5). And so Paul writes: "I determined not to know anything among you except Jesus Christ and Him crucified" (1 Cor. 2:2).

The minister of the gospel must never forget that it is for this especially that he has been set apart—to be with the Holy Spirit a witness for Christ. It is as he does this that sinners will find salvation and that God's children will be sanctified and fitted for His service. It is thus alone that Christ can have His place in the hearts of His people and in the world around.

But there is a second thought of no less importance. It is that the teaching must ever be a personal testimony from *experience* to what Christ is and can do. As this note is sounded, the Holy Spirit carries the message as a living reality to the heart. It is this that will build up believers so that they can walk in such fellowship with Jesus Christ that He can reveal Himself through them. And it is this that will lead them to the knowledge of the indispensable secret of spiritual health—a prayer life in daily fellowship, in childlike love, and in true consecration to the Father and the Son.

What abundant matter for a Prayer Union—to cultivate among believers and ministers that joy of the Holy Spirit in which, out of the abundance of the heart, the mouth speaks to the praise and glory of our ever-blessed Redeemer Jesus Christ our Lord.

Day 12

The Whole World

You shall be witnesses to Me . . . to the end of the earth.

Acts 1:8

HERE we have the fifth mark of Christ's church: *its aim—the whole world.*

What words are these for the man who in absolute impotence had been crucified by His enemies? How dare He speak of the ends of the earth as His dominion! What folly this reveals on the part of those who speak of Christ as being nothing but a man. How could it have entered the mind of any writer to venture the prophecy that a Jew who had been crucified, whose whole life had been proved by that cross to be an utter failure and whose disciples had at the last utterly forsaken Him—that by them He should conquer the world? No human mind could have formed such a conception. It is the thought of God; He alone could plan and execute such a purpose.

The word that Jesus spoke to His disciples, "You shall receive power when the Holy Spirit has come upon you" (Acts 1:8), gives them the assurance that the Holy Spirit would maintain in them Christ's divine power. As Christ did His works only because the Father worked in Him, so Christ assured His disciples that He Himself from the throne of heaven would work all their works in *them.* They might ask what they would and it should be done unto them. In the strength of that promise the church of Christ can make the ends of the earth its one aim.

Oh, that Christian people might understand that the extension of God's kingdom can only be effected by the united, continued prayer of men and women who give their hearts wholly to wait upon Christ in the assurance that what they desire He will do for them.

Oh, that God would grant that His children proved their faith in Christ by making His aim *their* aim—that they might yield themselves to be His witnesses in united, persevering prayer, waiting upon Him in full assurance that He will most surely and most graciously give all that they can ask.

My reader, do become one of those intercessors who really believe that in answer to your prayer the crucified Jesus will do far more than you can ask or think.

Day 13

The Whole Earth Filled with His Glory

Blessed be His glorious name forever! And let the whole earth be filled with His glory. Amen and Amen.

Psalm 72:19

WHAT a prospect! This earth, now so much under the power of the Evil One, renewed and *filled with the glory of God*—a new earth wherein righteousness dwells! Though we believe it so little, it will surely come to pass; God's Word is the pledge of it. God's Son by His blood and death conquered the power of sin, and through the eternal Spirit the power of God is working out His purpose. What a vision: the whole earth filled with His glory!

But what a mammoth and difficult work. It is nearly two thousand years since Christ gave the promise and ascended the throne, and more than one-half of the human race have yet even to hear of the name of Jesus. And among the other half, millions are called by His name yet know Him not. This great work of bringing the knowledge of Christ to every creature has been entrusted to a church that thinks little of her responsibility and of what the consequence of her neglect will be. We may indeed ask: Will the work ever be done? His power and His faithfulness are *pledges* that one day we shall see it, the whole earth filled with the glory of God! Blessed be His name!

What a wonderful prayer! For in our text it is a prayer—"Let the whole earth be filled with His glory. Amen and Amen." It is to this end that every believer is called, and he can count upon the Holy Spirit to inspire and to strengthen him. It is to this end that we desire to strengthen each other, so that every day of our life, with all the power there is in us, we with one accord and continually may pray in faith and in the name of Jesus and the power of His Spirit.

What blessedness to know that true prayer will indeed help—and be answered! What blessedness every day of our lives to seek God's face, with confidence to lay hold of Him and give Him no rest till the earth is full of His glory! Once again, what blessedness to unite with all God's willing children in this day of His power—with all who are seeking to prepare the way for our Kmg!

Day 14

The First Prayer Meeting

These all continued with one accord in prayer and supplication, with the women.

Acts 1:14

THE sixth mark of the early church: *waiting for the promise of the Father in united, unceasing prayer.* It is difficult to form a right conception of the unspeakable importance of this first prayer meeting in the history of the kingdom, a prayer meeting which was the simple fulfilling of the command of Christ. It was to be for all time the indication of the one condition through which His presence and Spirit would be known in power. In it we have the secret key that opens the storehouse of heaven with all its blessings.

Christ had prayed that the disciples might be one, even as He and the Father were one—*perfect* in one—that the world might know that God loved them as He loved Christ. How far the disciples were from such a state when Christ prayed the prayer we see in the strife that there was among them at the Lord's Table as to who would be chief. It was only after the resurrection, and after Christ had gone to heaven, that they would be brought, in the ten days of united supplication, to that holy unity of love and purpose which would make them the one body of Christ prepared to receive the Spirit in all His power.

What a prayer meeting! It was the fruit of Christ's training during His three years' companionship with them. Adam's body was created first, before God breathed the breath of life into him. And so the body of Christ had first to be formed before the Spirit took possession.

This prayer meeting gives us the law of the kingdom for all time. Where Christ's disciples are linked to each other in love and yield themselves wholly to Him in undivided consecration, the Spirit will be given from heaven as the seal of God's approval and Christ will show His mighty power. One of the great marks of the new dispensation is the united, unceasing prayer that avails much and is crowned with the power of the Holy Spirit. Have we not here the reason why, if our prayers are confined in great measure to our own church or interests, the answer cannot come in such power as we expected?

Day 15

The Unity of the Spirit

Endeavoring to keep the unity of the Spirit. . . . There is one body and one Spirit.

Ephesians 4:3–4

IT is from Paul that we learn how the Christian communities in different places ought to remember each other in the fellowship of prayer. He points out how in such prayer God is glorified. So he writes more than once (see 2 Cor. 1:11; 4:15; 9:12–13) of how the ministry of intercession abounds to the glory of God.

In our days there is very great need that the children of God throughout the world should be drawn close together in the consciousness of their being chosen by God to be a holy priesthood, ministering continually the sacrifice of praise and prayer. There is too little distinction between the world and the body of Christ in the life of many of God's children there is very little difference from what the world is. It is a question of the deepest importance: What can be done to foster the unity of the Spirit?

Nothing will help so much as the separation to a life of more prayer, with the definite intercession that God's people may prove their unity in a life of holiness and love. That will be a living testimony to the world of what it means to live for God. When Paul wrote: "Praying always with all prayer and supplication in the Spirit, being watchful to this end with all perseverance and supplication for all the saints" (Eph. 6:18), he named one of the essential characteristics of the difference between God's people and the world. You say you long to bear this mark of the children of God and to be able so to pray for them that you may prove to yourself and to others that you are indeed not of the world? Resolve in your life to bear about with you this one great distinctive feature of the true Christian—a life of intercession. Join with God's children who are seeking with one accord and unceasingly so to maintain the unity of the Spirit and the body of Christ that they may be strong in the Lord and in the power of His might—join with them to pray down a blessing upon His church. Let none of us think it too much to give a quarter of an hour every day for meditation on some word of God connected with His promises to His church—and then to plead with Him for its fulfillment. Slowly, unobservedly, and yet surely, you will taste the blessedness of being one, heart and soul, with God's people and receive the power to pray the effective prayer that avails much.

Day 16

Union Is Strength

And when they had prayed . . . they were all filled with the Holy Spirit, and they spoke the word of God with boldness. Now the multitude of those who believed were of one heart and one soul.

Acts 4:31–32

THE power of union we see everywhere in nature. How feeble is a drop of rain as it falls to earth. But when the many drops are united in one stream, and thus become one body, how speedily the power is irresistible. Such is the power of true union in prayer. In Psalm 34:5 the English margin has, instead of "They looked to Him," "They flowed to Him." The Dutch translation is, "They rushed towards Him like a stream of water." Such was the prayer in the upper room. And such can our prayer be if we unite all our forces in pleading the promise of the Father. And when the world "comes in like a flood," it can be overcome in the power of united prayer.

In Natal, owing to the many mountains, the streams often flow down with great force. The Zulus are accustomed, when they wish to pass through a stream, to join hands. The leader has a strong stick in the right hand and gives his left hand to some strong man who comes behind him. And so they form a chain of twelve or twenty and help each other to stem and cross the current. Let us believe that when in spirit God's people reach out their hands to each other, there will be power to resist the terrible influence that the world can exert. And in that unity God's children, when they have overcome the power of the world and the flesh, will have power to prevail with God.

It was in the upper room that they abode the ten days until they had truly become one heart and one soul. When the Spirit of God descended, He not only filled each individual but took possession of the whole company as the body of Christ.

Do believe, O Christians, that in this twentieth century the prayer of our Lord Jesus is still being offered: "Father . . . that they may be one as We *are*" (John 17:11). It is in the fellowship of loving and believing prayer that our hearts can be melted into one and that we shall become strong in faith to believe and to accept what God has promised us.

Day 17

Prayer in the Name of Christ

Whatever you ask in My name, that I will do, that the Father may be glorified in the Son.

John 14:13

HOW wonderful the link between our prayers and Christ's glorifying the Father in heaven. Much prayer on earth brings Him much glory in heaven. Little prayer means, as far as we are concerned, little glory to the Father. What an incentive to much prayer, to unceasing intercession. Our prayer is indispensable to the glorifying of the Father.

So deep was the desire of Christ in the last night that His disciples should learn to believe in the power of His name, and to avail themselves of His promise of a sure and abundant answer, that we find the promise repeated seven times over. He knew how slow men are to believe in the wonderful promise of answer to prayer in His name. He longs to rouse a large and confident faith, and to free our prayer from every shadow of a doubt, and to teach us to look upon intercession as the most certain and most blessed way of bringing glory to God, joy to our own souls, and blessing to the perishing world around us.

And if the thought comes to us that such prayer is not easily attained, we only need to remember what Christ told them. *It was when the Holy Spirit came that they would have power thus to pray.* It is to draw us on to yield ourselves fully to the control of the blessed Spirit that He holds out to us the precious promise: "Ask, and you will receive, that your joy may be full" (John 16:24). As we believe in the power of the Spirit working in us in full measure, intercession will become to us the joy and the strength of all our service.

When Paul wrote (Col. 3:17), "Whatever you do in word or deed, do all in the name of the Lord Jesus," he reminds us how in daily life everything is to bear the signature of Jesus. It is as we learn to do this that we shall have the confidence to say to the Father that, as we live in that name before men, we come to Him with the full confidence that our prayer in that name will be answered. The life in fellowship with men is to be one with the life in communion with God. It is when the name of Jesus rules all in our life that it will give power to our prayer also.

Day 18

Your Heavenly Father

Our Father in heaven.

Luke 11:2

HOW simple, how beautiful, this invocation which Christ puts upon our lips! And yet how inconceivably rich it is in its meaning, in the fullness of the love and blessing it contains.

Just think what a book could be written of all the memories that there have been on earth of wise and loving fathers. Just think of what this world owes to the fathers who have made their children strong and happy through giving their lives to seek the welfare of their fellow men. And then think how all this is but a shadow—a shadow of exquisite beauty, yet only a shadow—of what the Father in heaven is to His children on earth.

What a gift Christ bestowed on us when He gave us the right to say: "Father!" "The Father of Christ," "Our Father," "My Father."

And then, "Our Father in heaven," our heavenly Father. We count it a great privilege as we bow in worship to know that the Father comes near to us where we are upon earth. But we soon begin to feel the need of rising up to enter into His holy presence in heaven, to breathe its atmosphere, to drink in its spirit, and to become truly heavenly-minded. And as we in the power of thought and imagination leave earth behind, and in the power of the Holy Spirit enter the Holiest of All, where the seraphs worship the term "heavenly Father" takes on a new meaning, and our hearts come under an influence that can abide all the day.

And as we then gather up our thoughts of what fatherhood on earth has meant, and hear the voice of Christ saying: "How much more"—we feel the distance there is between the earthly picture and the heavenly reality, and can only bow in lowly, loving adoration, "Father, our Father, my Father." And only thus can full joy and power come to us as we rest rejoicingly in the word: "How much more will *your* heavenly Father give the Holy Spirit to those who ask Him!" (Luke 11:13).

Oh, for grace to cultivate a heavenly spirit, and daily to prove that we are children who have a Father in heaven and who love day by day to dwell in His holy presence!

The Power of Prayer

The effective, fervent prayer of a righteous man avails much.
James 5:16

PRAYER avails much. It avails much with God. It avails much in the history of His church and people. Prayer is the one great power which the church can exercise in securing the working of God's omnipotence in the world.

The prayer of a *righteous man* avails much. That is, a man who has the righteousness of Christ not only as a garment covering him but as a life-power inspiring him, as a new man "created . . . in righteousness and true holiness" (Eph. 4:24). A man who lives as a "slave of righteousness" (Rom. 6:16, 19). These are the righteous whom the Lord loves and whose prayer has power (see Ps. 66:18–19; 1 John 3:22). When Christ gave His great prayer promises in the last night, it was to those who keep His commandments. "If you love Me, keep My commandments. And I will pray the Father, and He will give you another Helper" (John 14:15–16). "If you keep My commandments, you will abide in My love. . . . You will ask what you desire, and it shall be done for you" (John 15:10, 7).

"The *effective, fervent prayer* of a righteous man avails much." It is only when the righteous man stirs up himself and rouses his whole being to take hold of God that the prayer avails much. As Jacob said, "I will not let You go" (Gen 32:26), as the importunate widow gave the unjust judge no rest—so it is that the effective, fervent prayer effects great things.

And then comes the effective, fervent prayer of *many* righteous. When two or three agree, there is the promise of an answer. How much more when hundreds and thousands unite with one accord to cry to God to display His mighty power on behalf of His people.

Let us join those who have united themselves to call upon God for the mighty power of the Holy Spirit in His church. What a great and blessed work, and what a sure prospect, in God's time, of an abundant answer! Let us pray God individually and unitedly for the grace of the effective, fervent prayer which avails much.

Day 20

Prayer and Sacrifice

I want you to know what a great conflict I have for you.
Colossians 2:1

AS men who are undertaking a great exploit have to prepare themselves and summon all their powers to their aid, so Christians need to prepare themselves to pray with their whole heart and strength (see Matt. 22:37). This is the law of the kingdom. Prayer needs sacrifice of ease, of time, of self. *The secret of powerful prayer is sacrifice.* It was thus with Christ Jesus, the great Intercessor. It is written of Him: "When You make His soul an offering for sin, He shall see His seed. . . . He shall divide the spoil with the strong, because He poured out His soul unto death" (Isa. 53:10, 12). In Gethsemane "He had offered up prayers and supplications, with vehement cries and tears" (Heb. 5:7). Prayer is *sacrifice*. David said: "Let my prayer be set before You as incense, the lifting up of my hands as the evening sacrifice" (Ps. 141:2).

Prayer is *based* on sacrifice. Our prayer has its worth alone from being rooted in the sacrifice of Jesus Christ. As He gave up everything in His prayer "Your will be done," our posture and disposition must ever be the offering up of everything to God and His service.

A pious Welsh miner had a relative whom the doctor ordered to Madeira for recuperation. But there was no money. The miner resolved to take the little money that he had and venture to use it all. He procured a comfortable lodging at 7s. 6d. per day for the invalid. He was content with an out-room for himself and lived on ten pence a day. He spent much time in prayer until he got the assurance that the invalid would recover. On the last day of the month the sick one was well. When the miner reached home, he said that he had now learned more than ever that the secret law and the hidden power of prayer lay in self-sacrifice.

Need we wonder at the lack of power in our prayer when there is so much reluctance to make the needful sacrifice in waiting upon God? Christ, the Christ we trust in, the Christ who lives in us, offered Himself as a sacrifice to God. It is as this spirit lives and rules in us that we shall receive power from Him as intercessors to pray the effective prayer that avails much.

Day 21

The Intercession of the Spirit for the Saints

He who searches the hearts knows what the mind of the Spirit is, because He makes intercession for the saints according to the will of God.

Romans 8:27

WHAT a light these words cast upon the life of prayer in the hearts of the saints! We know not what we should pray for as we ought. How often this hinders our prayer or hinders the faith that is essential to its success. But here we are told, for our encouragement, that the Holy Spirit makes intercession for us with groanings that cannot be uttered: "He makes intercession for the saints according to the will of God."

What a prospect is here opened up to us! Where and how does the Spirit make intercession for the saints? In no other way than that, in the heart which knows not what to pray, He secretly and effectively prays what is according to the will of God. This, of course, implies that we trust Him to do His work in us, and that we tarry before God even when we know not what to pray, in the assurance that the Holy Spirit is praying in us. This implies further that we take time to tarry in God's presence, that we exercise an unbounded dependence upon the Holy Spirit who has been given us to cry, "Abba, Father," within us, even when we have nothing to offer but groanings and sighs which cannot be verbalized.

What a difference it would make in the life of many of God's saints if they realized this! We have not only Jesus the Son of God, the great High Priest, ever living to intercede for us; we have not only the liberty of asking in faith what we desire and the promise that it shall be given us; but we have actually and in very deed the Holy Spirit, "the Spirit of grace and supplication" (Zech. 12:10), to carry on, in the depths of our being, His work of interceding for each of us according to the will of God.

What a call to separate ourselves from the world, to yield ourselves wholeheartedly to the leading and praying of the Spirit within us, deeper than all our thoughts or expectations! What a call to surrender ourselves in stillness of soul, resting in the Lord and waiting patiently for Him, as the Holy Spirit prays within us not only for ourselves but specially for all saints, according to the will of God!

Day 22

That They All May Be One

Holy Father, keep through Your name those whom You have given Me, that they may be one as We are. I do not pray for these alone, but also for those who will believe in Me through their word; that they all may be one, as You, Father, are in Me, and I in You; that they also may be one in Us. . . . And the glory which You gave Me I have given them, that they may be one just as We are one: I in them, and You in Me; that they may be made perfect in one, and that the world may know that You have sent Me.

John 17:11, 20–23

NOTICE carefully how the Lord uses the expression "*that they may be one*" five times over. It is as if He felt a need of laying the emphasis strongly upon these words if we are truly to realize the chief thought of His High Priestly Prayer.

He longs that the words and the thought shall in very deed have the same place in our hearts that they have in His. As He was on the way to go to the Father through the cross, He would have us understand that He took the thought and the desire with Him to heaven, to make it the object of His unceasing intercession there. And He entrusted the words to us that we should take them into the world with us and make them the object of our unceasing intercession.

That alone would enable us to fulfill the last, the new command, which He gave, that we should love the brethren as He loved us, so that our joy might be full.

How little the church has understood this. How little are its different branches marked by a fervent, affectionate love to all the saints of whatever name or denomination. Shall we not welcome heartily the invitation to make this prayer "*that they may be one*" a chief part of our daily fellowship with God? How simple it would be when once we connected the two words "Our Father" with all the children of God throughout the world. Each time we used these sacred words we would only have to expand this little word "Our" into all the largeness and richness of God's Father love, and our hearts would soon learn as naturally as we say "Father" with the thought of *His* infinite love and because of our love for *Him*, to say "Our" with childlike affection for all the saints of God, whoever and wherever they be. The prayer "*that they may be one*" would then become a joy and a strength, a deeper bond of fellowship with Christ Jesus and all His saints, and an offering with a sweet savor to the Father of love.

Day 23

The Disciples' Prayer

These all continued with one accord in prayer and supplication.

Acts 1:14

They continued steadfastly in . . . fellowship . . . and in prayers.

2:42

WHAT a lesson it would be for us in the school of prayer to have a clear apprehension of what this continuing with one accord in prayer meant to the disciples.

Just think of the object of their desire. However defective the thoughts were that they had of the blessed Spirit, they certainly knew, from the words of Jesus that "It is to your advantage that I go away" (John 16:7), that the Spirit would place the glorified Christ into their very hearts in a way they had never known Him before. And it would be He Himself, in the mighty power of God's Spirit, who would be their strength for the work to which He had called them.

With what confidence they expected the fulfillment of the promise! Had not the Master, who had loved them so well, given them the assurance of what He would send upon them from the throne of the Father in heaven?

And with what intensity and persistency they pleaded. In the midst of the praise and thanksgiving that filled their hearts as they worshiped their Lord in heaven, they prayed remembering all He had taught them about importunity, in full assurance that however long the answer might be delayed, He would most assuredly fulfill their desires. Let us nourish our hearts with thoughts such as these, until we realize that the very same promise that was given to the disciples is given to us, and that *we too*, even though we have to cry day and night to God, can count upon the Father to answer our prayers.

And then—and this is not the least—let us believe that as they continued with one accord in prayer, we also may unite as one in presenting our petitions, even though we cannot be together in one place. We can—in the love wherewith His Spirit makes us one, and in the experience of our Lord's presence with each one who joins with His brethren in pleading the blessed name—we can claim the promise that we, too, shall be filled with the Holy Spirit.

Day 24

Paul's Call to Prayer

Praying always with all prayer and supplication in the Spirit, being watchful to this end with all perseverance and supplication for all the saints—and for me.

Ephesians 6:18–19

WHAT a sense Paul had of the deep, divine unity of the whole body of Christ and of the actual need of unceasing prayer for all the members of the body by all who belong to it. That he did not mean this to be an occasional thing, but the unceasing exercise of the life union in. which they were bound together, is evident from the words he uses: "Praying always with *all prayer* and supplication in the Spirit, being watchful to this end with *all perseverance* and supplication *for all the saints.*" He expects believers to be so filled with the consciousness of their being in Christ, and through Him united consciously to the whole body, that in their daily life and all its engagements their highest aim would ever be the welfare of the body of Christ of which they had become members. He counted upon their being filled with the Spirit, so that it would be perfectly natural to them, without the thought of burden or constraint, to pray for all who belong to the body of Jesus Christ. As natural as it is for each member of my body to be ready every moment to do what is needful for the welfare of the whole, even so, where the Holy Spirit has entire possession, the consciousness of union with Christ will ever be accompanied by consciousness of the union and the joy and the love of all the members.

Is not this just what we need in our daily life, that every believer who has yielded himself undividedly to Christ Jesus shall day by day, every day, and all the day, live in the consciousness that he is one with Christ and His body? Just as this war has brought to light the intensity and the readiness with which millions of the subjects of the King sacrifice their all for the King and his service, so the saints of God shall live for Christ *their* King, and for all the members of that body of which He is the Head. May God's people be willing to offer this sacrifice of prayer and intercession at all times and for all saints!

Day 25

Paul's Request for Prayer

And for me, that utterance may be given to me, that I may open my mouth boldly to make known the mystery of the gospel . . . that in it I may speak boldly, as I ought to speak.
Ephesians 6:19–20

"AND for me"—what light these words cast on the deep reality of Paul's faith in the absolute necessity and the wonderful power of prayer. Just listen to what he asks that they should pray for: "That utterance may be given to me, that I may open my mouth boldly . . . that in it I may speak boldly, as I ought to speak."

Paul had now been a minister of the gospel for more than twenty years. One would assume that he had such experience of preaching and utterance that it would come naturally to him to speak boldly as he ought to speak. But so deep is his conviction of his own insufficiency and weakness, so absolute is his dependence on divine teaching and power, that he feels that without the direct help of God he cannot do the work as it ought to be done. The sense of his total and unalterable dependence upon God, who was with him, teaching him what and how to speak, is the ground of all his confidence and the keynote of his whole life. But there is more. He had in all these twenty years, times without number, been in circumstances where he had to throw himself upon God alone, with no one to help him in prayer. And yet, such is his deep spiritual insight into the unity of the body of

Christ and of his own actual dependence on the prayers of others, that he pleads for their praying with all prayer and supplication in the Spirit, and watching thereunto with all perseverance, and asks that they shall not forget to pray for him. As little as a wrestler can afford to dispense with the help of the weakest member of his body in the struggle in which he is engaged, so little could Paul do without the prayers of the believers.

What a call to us in this twentieth century, to awake to the consciousness that Christ, our Intercessor *in heaven*, and all saints here *upon earth*, are engaged in one mighty contest, and that it is our duty to call out and to cultivate the gift of unceasing supplication for the power of God's Spirit in all His servants, that all may have divine utterance given them, and that all may speak boldly and as they ought to speak.

Day 26

Prayer for All Saints

To the saints and faithful brethren in Christ who are in Colosse: . . . We give thanks to the God and Father of our Lord Jesus Christ, praying always for you, since we heard . . . of your love for all the saints. . . . Continue earnestly in prayer, being vigilant in it with thanksgiving; meanwhile praying also for us.

Colossians 1:2–4; 4:2–3

PRAYER for all the saints: let this be our first thought. It will need time, and thought, and love, to realize what is included in that simple expression. Think of your own neighborhood and the saints you know; think of your whole country, and praise God for all who are His saints; think of the Christian nations of the world, and the saints to be found in each of these; think of all the heathen nations and the saints of God to be found among them in ever-increasing numbers.

Think of all the different circumstances and conditions in which these are to be found and all the greatly varying needs which call for God's grace and help. Think of many, oh, so many, who are God's saints, and yet through ignorance or sloth, through worldly-mindedness or an evil heart of unbelief, are walking in the dark and bringing no honor to God. Think of so many who are in earnest and yet conscious of a life of failure, with little or no power to please God or to bless man. And then think again of those who are to be found everywhere, in solitary places or in companies, whose one aim is to serve the Lord who bought them. Think of them especially as joining, often unconscious of their relation to the whole body of Christ, in pleading for the great promise of the Holy Spirit and the love and oneness of heart which He alone can give.

This is not the work of one day or one night. It requires a heart which will set itself from time to time to do serious thinking in regard to the state and the needs of the body of Christ to which we belong. But when once we begin, we shall find what abundant reason there is for our persevering and yielding to God's Spirit, so that He may fit us for the great and blessed work of day by day praying a twofold prayer: for the love of God and Christ to fill the hearts of His people, and for the power of the Holy Spirit to come down and accomplish God's work in this sinful world.

Prayer by All Saints

We trust [in God] that He will still deliver us, you also helping together in prayer for us.

Second Corinthians 1:10–11

[Some] preach Christ from selfish ambition, not sincerely, supposing to add affliction to my chains. . . . I know that this will turn out for my deliverance through your prayer and the supply of the Spirit of Jesus Christ.

Philippians 1:16, 19

THIS subject calls us once again to think of all saints throughout the world but leads us to view them from a different standpoint. When we ask God to increase the number and the power of those who pray, we shall be given some impression of what the hope is that our circle of intercessors may gradually increase in number and power.

Our first thoughts will naturally turn to the multitude of the saints who think and know very little about the duty or the blessedness of pleading for the body of Christ, or for all the work which has to be done to perfect its members. We shall then have to remember how many there are—for whom we may praise God—that do intercede for the power of His Spirit, but their thoughts are chiefly limited to spheres of work that they are acquainted with or directly interested in.

That will leave us with what is, comparatively speaking, the very limited number of those who might be ready to take part in the specific prayer which ought to be sent up by the whole church—for the unity of the body and the power of the Spirit. And even then the number may be but small who really feel themselves drawn and urged to take part in this daily prayer for the outpouring of the Spirit on all God's people.

And yet many may be feeling that the proposal meets a long-felt need, and that it is an unspeakable privilege, whether with few or many, to make Christ's last prayer, "*that they may be one*" (John 17:11), the daily supplication of our faith and love. It may be that in time believers will band together in small circles, or throughout wider districts, in helping to rouse those around them to take part in the great work, that the prayer *for all saints* may become one *by all saints*.

This message is sent out as a broadcast to all hearts that desire to be in touch with it, with the hope of increasing their consecration to their Lord in the matter of unceasing daily supplication for the power of His love and Spirit to be revealed to *all* His people.

Day 28

Prayer for All the Fullness of the Spirit

"Bring all the tithes into the storehouse . . . and try Me now in this," says the Lord *of hosts, "if I will not open for you the windows of heaven and pour out for you such blessing that there will not be room enough to receive it."*

Malachi 3:10

THIS last promise in the Old Testament tells us how *abundant* the blessing is to be—beyond our capacity to receive it! Pentecost was only the *beginning* of what God was willing to do. The promise of the Father, as Christ gave it, still waits for its perfect fulfillment. Let us try to realize what liberty we have to ask and expect great things.

Just as the great command to go and preach the gospel was not only meant for the disciples but for us too, so the very last command, "Tarry . . . until you are endued with power from on high—Wait for the Promise of the Father . . . [for] you shall be baptized with the Holy Spirit" (Luke 24:49; Acts 1:4–5), is also for us. It is the ground for our confident assurance that our prayer with one accord will be heard.

Take time to think of what a cry of need there is throughout the whole church and throughout all our mission fields. Let us realize that the only remedy to be found for inefficiency or impotence, to enable us to gain the victory over the powers of this world or of darkness, is in the manifested presence of our Lord in the midst of His hosts and in the power of His Spirit.

Let us take time to think of the state of the various churches throughout Christendom. We will be brought deeper than ever to the conviction that nothing can avail except the supernatural, almighty intervention of our Lord Himself. He must rouse His hosts for the great battle against evil. Can anyone conceive or suggest any other matter for prayer that can at all compete with this: for the power of God on the ministers of the gospel, and on all His people, to endue them with power from on high to make the gospel in very deed the power of God unto salvation?

As we connect the prayer for the whole church on earth with the prayer for the whole power of God in heaven, we shall feel that the greatest truths of the heavenly world and the kingdom of God have possession of us, and that we are in very deed asking what God is longing to give, as soon as He finds hearts utterly yielded to Himself in faith and obedience.

Day 29

Every Day

Give us day by day our daily bread.

Luke 11:3

THERE are some Christians who are afraid of making a promise to pray for others every day. To make such a commitment is altogether beyond them—they could not undertake it. And yet they pray to God to give them their bread day by day. Surely if a child of God has once yielded himself with his whole life to God's love and service, he should count it a privilege to avail himself of any invitation that would help him *every day* to come into God's presence with the great need of His church and kingdom.

Are there not many who confess that they desire to live wholly for God? They acknowledge that Christ gave Himself for them and works in them without ceasing. They admit the claim that nothing less than the measure of the love of Christ to us is to be the measure of our love to Him. They feel that if this is indeed to be the standard of their lives, they ought surely to welcome every opportunity for proving day by day that they are devoting their heart's strength to the interests of Christ's kingdom and to the prayer that can bring down God's blessing.

Our invitation to daily united prayer may come to some as a new and perhaps unexpected opportunity of becoming God's remembrancers who cry day and night for His power and blessing on His people and on this needy world. Think of the privilege of being thus allowed to plead every day with God on behalf of His saints, for the outpouring of His Spirit, and for the coming of His kingdom—that His will may indeed be done on earth as it is in heaven. To those who have to confess that they have but little understood the high *privilege* and the solemn *duty* of waiting on God in prayer for His blessing on the world, the invitation ought to be most welcome. And even to those who have already their special circles of work for which to pray, the thought that the enlargement of their vision, and their hearts, to include *all God's saints* and *all the work of His kingdom*, and *all the promise of an abundant outpouring of His Spirit*, should urge them to take part in a ministry by which their other work will not suffer but their hearts will be strengthened with a joy and a love and a faith that they have never known before.

Day 30

With One Accord

They were all with one accord in one place. . . . And they were all filled with the Holy Spirit.

Acts 2:1, 4

OUR last chapters have opened to us wonderful thoughts about the solidarity of the whole body of Christ and have shown the need for deliberate cultivation of the slumbering or buried talents of intercession. We may indeed thank God, for we know of tens of thousands of His children who in daily prayer are pleading specially for some portion of the work of God's kingdom in which they are personally interested. But in many cases the prayers are *limited* to the work that they take an interest in, and there is a lack of that large-hearted and universal love that takes up *all* the saints of God and their service into its embrace. There is not the boldness and the strength that comes from the consciousness of being part of a large and conquering army under the leadership of our conquering King.

We said that a wrestler in the games gathers up his whole strength and counts upon every member of his body doing its very utmost. In the British Army in the present war, with its millions of soldiers, each detachment not only throws its whole heart into the work that it has to do, but it is ready to rejoice and take new courage from every tiding of the bravery and enthusiasm of the far-distant members of the one great army. And is not this what we need in the church of Christ—such an enthusiasm for the King and His kingdom, and such a faith in His purpose that His name shall be made known to every human being, that our prayers shall rise up every day with a large-hearted love that grasps the whole body of Christ and pleads daily for the power of the Holy Spirit on all its members, even to the very feeblest?

The strength unity gives is something inconceivable. The power of each individual member is increased to a large degree by the inspiration of fellowship with a large and conquering host. Nothing can so help us to an ever-larger faith as the consciousness of being one body and one spirit in Christ Jesus. It was as the disciples were all with one accord in one place on the Day of Pentecost that they were all filled with the Holy Spirit. United prayer brings the answer to prayer.

Day 31

A Personal Call

We should not trust in ourselves but in God . . . who delivered us . . . and . . . will still deliver us.

Second Corinthians 1:9–10

[Some] preach Christ from selfish ambition, not sincerely, supposing to add affliction to my chains. . . . I know that this will turn out for my deliverance through your prayer and the supply of the Spirit of Jesus Christ.

Philippians 1:16, 19

TEXTS like these prove that there were still Christians in the churches under the full power of the Holy Spirit, on whom Paul could count for effective, much-availing prayer. When we plead with Christians to pray without ceasing, there are a very large number who quietly decide that such a life is not possible for them. They do not have any special gift for prayer; they lack the intense desire for glorifying Christ in the salvation of souls; they have not yet learned what it is, under the power of the constraining love of Christ, to live not unto themselves but unto Him who died for them and rose again.

And yet it is to such that we bring this call to offer themselves for a wholehearted surrender to live entirely for Christ. We ask them whether they are not ashamed of the selfish life that simply uses Christ as a convenience to escape from hell and to secure a place in heaven. We come to them with the assurance that God can change their lives and fill their hearts with Christ and His Holy Spirit. We plead with them to believe that with God all things are possible. He is able and willing, yea rather most anxious, to restore them to the Father's house, to the joy of His presence and service.

One step on the way to the attainment of this will be that they listen to the call for men and women who will, every day and all the day, in the power of Christ's abiding presence, live in the spirit of unceasing intercession for all saints—that they receive the power of the Holy Spirit, and acknowledge that this is nothing less than a duty, a sacrifice that Christ's love has a right to claim, and that He by His Spirit will indeed work in them. Any believer, however far he may have come short, who accepts the call as coming from Christ and draws near to God in humble prayer for the needed grace, will have taken the first step on the path that leads to fellowship with God, to a new faith and life in Christ Jesus, and to the surrender of his whole being to that intercession of the Spirit that will help to bring Pentecost again into the hearts of God's people.

CLC PUBLICATIONS

Fort Washington, PA 19034

This book is published by CLC Publications, an outreach of CLC Ministries International. The purpose of CLC is to make evangelical Christian literature available to all nations so that people may come to faith and maturity in the Lord Jesus Christ. We hope this book has been life changing and has enriched your walk with God through the work of the Holy Spirit. If you would like to know more about CLC, we invite you to visit our website:

www.clcusa.org

To know more about the remarkable story of the founding of CLC International we encourage you to read

LEAP OF FAITH

Norman Grubb

Paperback

Size 5¼ x 8, Pages 248

ISBN: 978-0-87508-650-7

ISBN (e-book): 978-1-61958-055-8

THE SECRET OF POWER FROM ON HIGH

Andrew Murray

Have you learned the secret to a life that is wholly surrendered to the leading of the Holy Spirit? Part of Andrew Murray's classic *Secret Series* devotionals, *The Secret of Power from On High* simply presents how to exercise the great privilege of close fellowship with God in prayer through the Holy Spirit and the meaning of a life of all-prevailing intercession.

Paperback
Size 4¹/₄ x 7, Pages 69
ISBN: 978-1-61958-268-2
ISBN (*e-book*): 978-1-61958-269-9

THE SECRET OF THE FAITH LIFE

Andrew Murray

How can a feeble faith in an almighty Christ move mountains? Part of Andrew Murray's classic *Secret Series* devotionals, *The Secret of the Faith Life* provides insight into the need, power, and blessedness of a wholehearted faith in Jesus and an unreserved surrender to Him, so that we can be prepared to receive Him in the fullness of His love and abiding presence.

Paperback
Size 4 1/4 x 7, Pages 69
ISBN: 978-1-61958-270-5
ISBN (*e-book*): 978-1-61958-271-2

THE SECRET OF ADORATION

Andrew Murray

The Secret Series books contain a wealth of teaching that is based on Andrew Murray's mature and full experience in Christ. *The Secret of Adoration* contains one month of daily selections that highlight the importance of true worship in the lives of believers.

Paperback
Size 4¹/₄ x 7, Pages 71
ISBN: 978-1-61958-253-8
ISBN (*e-book*): 978-1-61958-254-5

THE SECRET OF INTERCESSION

Andrew Murray

The Secret Series books contain a wealth of teaching that is based on Andrew Murray's mature and full experience in Christ. *The Secret of Intercession* contains one month of daily selections that reveal the power of intercession.

Paperback
Size $4^{1}/_{4}$ x 7, Pages 67
ISBN: 978-1-61958-249-1
ISBN (*e-book*): 978-1-61958-250-7

THE SECRET OF THE ABIDING PRESENCE

Andrew Murray

The Secret Series books contain a wealth of teaching that is based on Andrew Murray's mature and full experience in Christ. *The Secret of the Abiding Presence* contains one month of daily selections that reveal the peace that comes with resting in the presence of God.

Paperback
Size 4¼ x 7, Pages 67
ISBN: 978-1-61958-251-4
ISBN (*e-book*): 978-1-61958-252-1